SCIENCE ALIVE
All Around

Robin Kerrod

Series consultant:
Professor Eric Laithwaite

Educational consultant:
Dr Helen Rapson

Subject consultant:
Iain Bain

 Silver Burdett Press

How to use this book

There are four books in the **Science Alive** series: **Moving Things**, **Changing Things**, **Living Things**, and **All Around**. They will introduce you to science in the world around you.

To find information, first look at the contents page opposite. Read the chapter list. It tells you what each page is about. You can then find the page with the information you need.

The colors on the contents page will help you to find your way through the book. Each main topic in the book is shown by a colored stripe that matches the color around the edges of the pages about that topic.

On each pair of pages inside the book, you will see this in the top right hand corner:

This shows you where to find out more about the subjects covered in those two pages. The signs tell you which of the four Science Alive books and which pages to look at.

 is the symbol for Moving Things,

 for Changing Things,

 for Living Things,

 for All Around.

You can see the symbol on the cover of each book.

For example, pages 8-9 of this book are about the atmosphere, and have these signs:

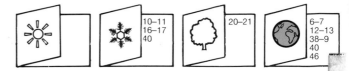

These mean: to find out more about the atmosphere, look at pages 10-11, 16-17, and 40 of Changing Things, pages 20-21 of Living Things, and pages 6-7, 12-13, 38-39, 40, and 46 of this book.

On pages 37-52 of this book there are some simple activities and experiments you can try. There is a separate contents list of those on page 37, and they will help you to understand and find out more about the information in the rest of this book.

If you want to know about one particular thing, look it up in the index on page 54. For example, if you want to know about hydro-electricity, the index tells you that there is something about it on pages 15 and 53. The index also lists the pictures in the book.

When you read this book, you will find some unusual words. The first time each one is used it is written in **dark** letters. The glossary on page 53 explains what these words mean.

CONTENTS

EARTH AND AIR

The Earth

Can you stand on a ball without falling off? There is one ball you can stand on easily, because it is so big. It is the ball we live on, which we call the Earth.

Some of the Earth is covered with land, but most of it is covered with water. We call the big areas of land the **continents**, and the big areas of water the oceans, or seas. The continent we live on is called North America. The Atlantic Ocean is to the east and the Pacific to the west.

The garden is part of a bigger area of land, maybe in a town like this.

Where do you live? It may be in an apartment building, or in a house like this, with a garden around it.

Each country is part of
one of the continents on
the Earth's surface.

The land on which each
town stands is part of an
even bigger area of land,
or country.

All around the Earth there is a layer
of **air**, which we call the **atmosphere**.
When we go above the atmosphere, we
are in **Space**. So the Earth is a huge
ball of rock, water, and other things,
surrounded by atmosphere and moving
in Space.

The atmosphere

We can't see the atmosphere – the layer of air around the Earth – so how do we know it's there? One way we know is because we can feel it. Take a deep breath. Can you feel the air rushing into your mouth? When a lot of air is moving, we call it the wind.

We could not live without the atmosphere. People, animals, and plants all need the air in the atmosphere to stay alive. Air is a mixture of different gases. The gas that we use to keep us alive is called **oxygen**. Our bodies take it from the air when we breathe.

This picture of clouds in the atmosphere was taken from a spacecraft. Clouds are made from water vapor which has cooled and changed into tiny drops of water.

The Moon has no atmosphere, so astronauts take air with them.

Another gas in the air is **water vapor**. This is water that has turned into gas. The more water vapor there is in the air, the wetter the weather will be.

The atmosphere spreads high above the Earth for hundreds of miles. But it changes as it goes up. It is thickest near the ground and gets thinner as it goes higher. It is hard to breathe properly at the top of high mountains because there is not enough air in the atmosphere up there. The atmosphere goes on getting thinner and thinner far above the mountains until there is nothing left. This is where Space begins. In Space, there is no air at all.

Flying

Have you ever flown in an airplane? If you have, there were probably lots of other people on it, too. A plane with all those people on it is very heavy. How can such a heavy thing stay up in the air? It stays up because the air pushes it up. Birds stay up in the air the same way.

Can you think of something that birds and planes both have? They both have **wings**, and so do all things that fly. It is their wings that keep them up in the air.

A hang-glider has no engines and moves slowly. The big wings help to keep it and the person up in the air.

glider

swallow

The swallow and the glider have long, tapered wings for gliding. The curve of the swallow's wings help it travel fast.

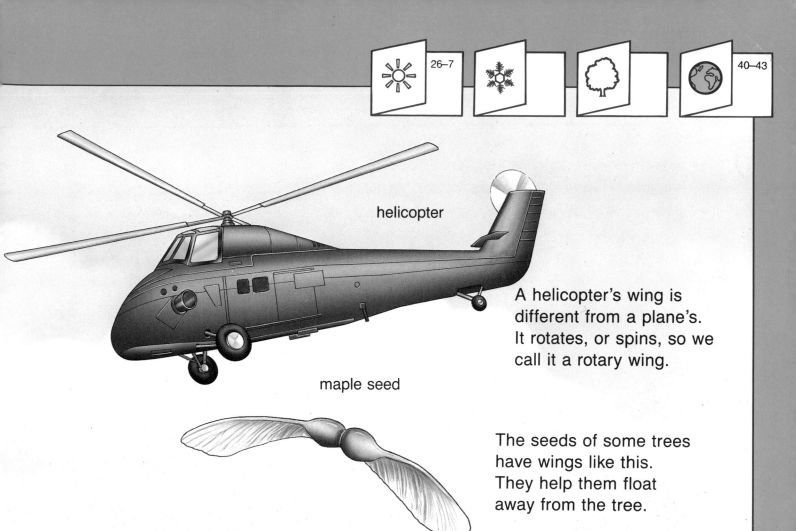

helicopter

A helicopter's wing is different from a plane's. It rotates, or spins, so we call it a rotary wing.

maple seed

The seeds of some trees have wings like this. They help them float away from the tree.

Try this experiment to see how wings work. Hold a tray in front of you, and lift up the front a little. Now run as fast as you can, and you will find that the air pushes the tray up. By moving through the air, you have made the tray lift up.

The same kind of thing happens with a plane. To take off, its engines move it along the runway. As it goes faster, the air pushes up more and more on its wings. Soon the push of the air is so strong that it lifts the plane off the ground, and the plane starts to fly.

A bird rises into the air in the same way. The bird's wings are also its "engine." The bird flaps its wings against the air, and the air pushes the bird forward.

An insect beats the air with its frail wings. The wings keep it up in the air and push it forward.

11

WEATHER AND SEASONS

The weather

What is the weather going to be like tomorrow? The easiest way to find out is to look at the weather forecast on television.

The weather forecast tells you about tomorrow's temperature – how hot or cold it will be. It tells you if there will be any wind, and whether it will rain or snow. It may even show you pictures of the world taken from Space. These show how the clouds are moving. The clouds are carried along by the wind.

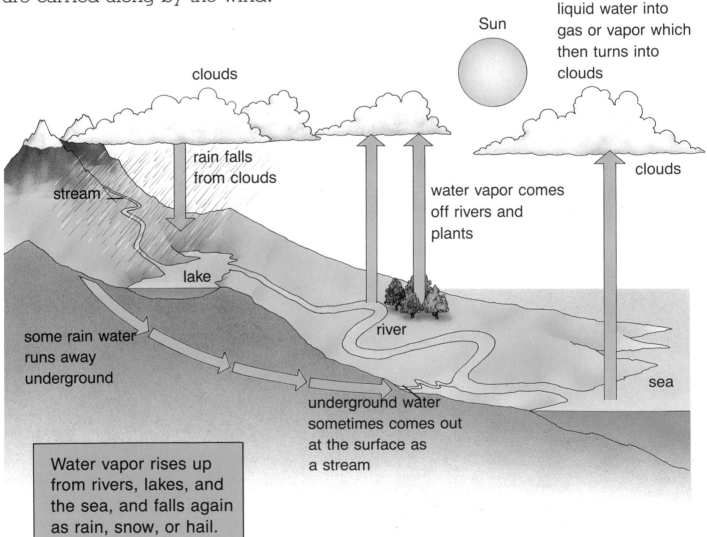

Sun's heat turns liquid water into gas or vapor which then turns into clouds

Sun

clouds

rain falls from clouds

stream

water vapor comes off rivers and plants

clouds

lake

river

some rain water runs away underground

sea

underground water sometimes comes out at the surface as a stream

Water vapor rises up from rivers, lakes, and the sea, and falls again as rain, snow, or hail.

The kind of weather we have depends a lot on which way the wind blows. Winds from the north or west often bring cold weather. Winds blowing in from the ocean often bring rain.

The winds passing over the ocean pick up water vapor rising from below. When the vapor cools, it turns into tiny drops of water which gather to make clouds. The drops may join up and get so big and heavy that they fall from the clouds, and it starts to rain.

If it is very cold, water vapor freezes straight from gas to solid ice, making snow flakes. But if the drops of water in the clouds freeze, they turn into hail.

When it does not rain for a long time, we say there is a drought. During a drought, reservoirs may dry up.

On the coast the wind blows in from the sea much of the time. It often bends trees into weird shapes.

Power from the weather

Have you ever tried to ride a bicycle in the wind? It is hard to cycle against the wind, but easy when the wind is behind you. You can feel how strong the wind is.

A really strong wind can cause a lot of damage. It can uproot trees, toss cars into the air, and blow down buildings. But the wind can be a friend as well as an enemy. We can use its power to move things and to drive machines. We can use it to blow the sails on sail boats, and make the boats move.

At sea, the wind whips up the waves and makes them crash against the shore. Scientists are trying to find ways of using wave power to make electricity.

Sun's heat

solar panels let heat in but stop it from escaping

The force of a hurricane wind can blow down trees and buildings, and cause huge waves.

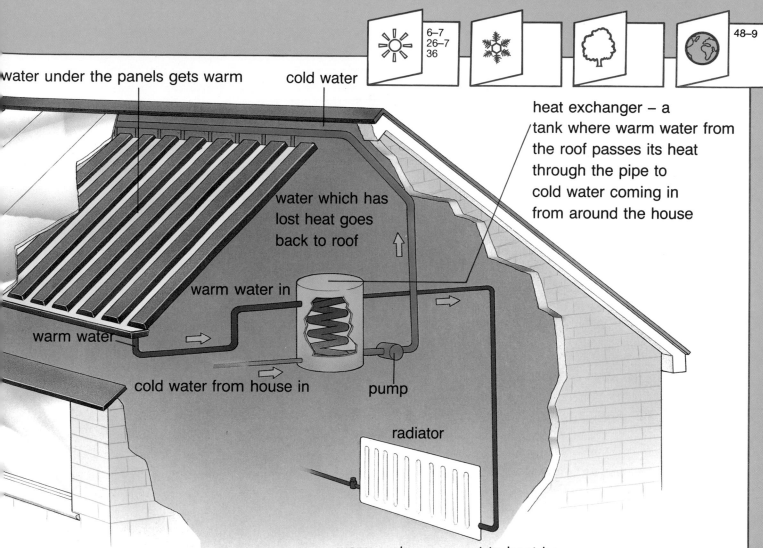

water under the panels gets warm

cold water

6–7
26–7
36

48–9

heat exchanger – a tank where warm water from the roof passes its heat through the pipe to cold water coming in from around the house

water which has lost heat goes back to roof

warm water in

warm water

cold water from house in

pump

radiator

warm water goes out to heat house

In some places, we build dams across rivers. Then we use the water that flows from the dam to drive machines that make electricity. We call this **hydro-electricity**. "Hydro" means "water."

We can also use the heat of the Sun to make things work. We call this **solar power**. "Solar" means "of the Sun." Some houses use solar power to heat their water. They trap the heat of the Sun with special panels. The water in swimming pools can be heated in this way, too. Most spacecraft also work on solar power, using sunlight to make electricity.

Solar power, from the Sun, can be used to heat houses. Sunlight can also be used to make electricity.

The seasons

What time of the year do you like best? You will probably say summer. In summer, the weather is usually warm and sunny, and it also stays light for a long time. In the far north of the world, the sky stays light all night.

In winter, the weather is much colder, and the days are much shorter. In the middle of winter, it gets dark before 5 o'clock in the afternoon.

Why do these changes happen? It is because of the way the Earth is tilted, or leans. While moving around the Sun in summer, our part of the Earth is leaning closer towards the Sun, so we get more of its heat and light.

Many parts of the world have four seasons. In winter, it is cold, and many trees and other plants seem dead. But they are not dead, and once the weather warms up in spring, they shoot into life again. Birds and other wild creatures become active again and have families.

30°F

55°F

In winter, the Earth has traveled halfway around the Sun. Then our part is tilted away from the Sun, and we get less heat and light.

Winter and summer are times of the year we call **seasons**. There are two other seasons, spring and autumn. Spring comes after winter. This is when the weather starts to get warmer, the days get longer, and flowers and other plants start to grow again. Autumn comes after summer. The weather gets cooler, the days get shorter, leaves fall from the trees, and some birds fly to warmer places. Spring, summer, autumn, and winter come and go every year.

The weather is hottest in the summer. The flowers are in full bloom, and the air is full of buzzing insects. The weather becomes cooler as autumn comes. Leaves start to fall from the trees, and living things prepare for the cold months of winter.

75°F

50°F

Climate

The kind of weather we have changes as the seasons change, but the seasons themselves stay more or less the same. The weather next spring will be much the same as it was last spring. Next winter will be much the same as last winter, and so it is with all the seasons.

The kind of weather we have during the year is called our **climate**. Our country has one kind of climate. Countries in other parts of the world have different climates. The weather they have during the year is different from ours.

Countries near the **Equator**, or middle of the Earth, have the hottest climate. We call it tropical. It is very hot and it rains a lot. Because of this, plants grow quickly and all through the year.

The hottest and wettest parts of the world are near the equator. Here plants grow quickly and all through the year.

Near the North and South Poles, the weather is bitterly cold all through the year. Hardly any plants can grow there.

Away from the Equator, there are places which are still very hot, but have hardly any rain. They are the **deserts**. Not many plants can grow in a desert climate because there is not enough water to keep them alive.

Farther away from the Equator, the climate gets cooler and wetter again. The summers are warm or even hot, and the winters are cool and rainy. Plants grow, flower, and fruit depending on what the season is.

The North and South **Poles**, at the top and bottom of the Earth, have the coldest climates of all. It is cold there all year long, and it is also very dry. Few plants can grow there.

The changing landscape

When you go outside after a heavy rainstorm, you will often see little streams of water running across the paths and roads. Look at them carefully. As well as water, they carry with them bits of dirt and little stones. They have washed these away from the ground as they passed over it.

When a stream runs over the ground for a long time, it slowly wears away a channel. In time, the channel gets deeper and wider. As other streams join it, the stream becomes a river and wears away a valley in the land. This is one way in which the weather changes the land around us, the landscape.

These pictures show the same part of Mexico City before and after a big earthquake in 1985. The tall skyscrapers and office buildings fell down when the ground shook beneath them.

The howling wind and the lashing rain have shaped these rocks into great arches. In time the rocks will be completely worn away.

The weather can also make holes in roads. In winter, water seeps into the little cracks and holes in the road that you don't normally see. If it gets cold enough, the water freezes into ice. Water expands, or gets bigger, when it turns to ice, so the ice makes the holes and cracks in the road bigger.

The same thing happens in the mountains in winter. Water seeps into cracks in the rocks, freezes, and starts to break up the rock.

The rocks and cliffs at the seashore wear away, too. As the waves crash in, they break up the rocks. There is sand in the waves and this helps to grind the rocks away even more. In time, the rocks themselves will be ground down to sand.

People change the landscape when they farm crops. Here, farmers have cut down the rain forest to make fields to grow rice.

21

Power from inside the Earth

A very long time ago, the Earth was quite different from the way it is now. The weather was warm, and huge swamps covered the Earth. Large trees and ferns grew in these swamps.

When the trees and ferns died, they fell to the ground and began to rot. Later, rivers and seas washed over them and covered them with mud and sand. The mud and sand were heavy and they pressed down on the layer of plants. They squashed it so much that it finally turned into the hard, black stuff we call **coal**.

Coal is a good **fuel**. It makes a lot of heat when we burn it. Most of the coal we mine, or take from the ground, goes to power stations. They burn the coal to heat water which changes to steam, and it drives machines that make electricity.

In some parts of the world, water deep underground in the hot part of the Earth becomes steam. The steam is piped to the surface to heat buildings and to drive machines that make electricity.

coal is loaded onto trains

washing and sorting plant

coal cutter at coal face

conveyor belt carries coal to elevator shaft

Coal is found underground in layers, or seams, and is reached by mining.

elevator carries coal to the sur

Oil is another fuel we get from under the ground or the sea. Oil was made in the same way as coal, from rotting sea plants and animals that were covered with mud and sand.

Some of the oil was trapped in rocks. Today we drill holes to reach it. Sometimes we also find gas, which was made at the same time as the oil. We call this **natural gas**. Power stations burn oil and gas to make electricity. At home, people use them for heating and cooking.

In some countries, people use steam from under the ground to heat their houses or to make electricity. The steam comes from water which hot rocks have heated. The steam sometimes pushes the water up out of the ground in huge, hot fountains called geysers.

Much of the world's oil comes from under the deserts of the Middle East. At this oil well, gas coming up with the oil is burned off.

Natural resources

The Earth gives us everything we need to live. We call these things **natural resources**. Air, water, and soil are three important natural resources. All living things need air and water to stay alive. Plants need soil to grow in, and we need plants for food.

Coal, oil, and natural gas are also important natural resources. We get them from under the ground and burn them as fuel in our homes and factories.

We use some natural resources to make other things. We use the wood from forests to build houses and make furniture. We use the **minerals** which we dig from the ground to make metals and chemicals. We can make plastics, paints, and dyes from oil and natural gas, as well as using them for fuel.

In some places coal is found on or near the surface. Then it can be mined more easily using huge power machines, but this makes the landscape look ugly.

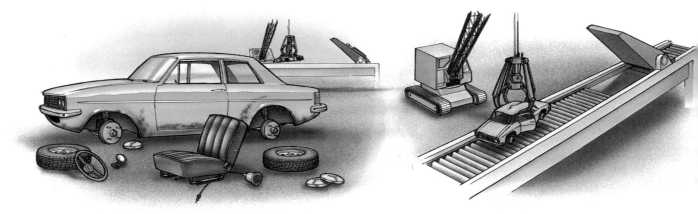

Some parts of an old car can be used again.

The rest of the car goes to a scrapyard.

Every day, we all use up some natural resources, or things made from them. Look in your trash can at the end of the week and see how much garbage your family has thrown away. Think how much garbage all the families in the world throw away each week!

To make some of the things that the world throws away, millions of trees have to be cut down, millions of gallons of fuel have to be burned, and millions of tons of minerals have to be mined. If we are not careful, we will soon use them all up. We must look after our resources and not waste them.

We can save some things by recycling them. This means using them again. In some countries, people already recycle paper, glass, and metals.

At the scrapyard the car body is crushed.

The crushed metal is melted again in a furnace.

Our world

The early people on Earth had to live on whatever they could find around them. They ate wild berries and roots and hunted wild animals for food. They found pieces of stone, bone, and wood and used these to make tools and weapons. They used wood fires for cooking and warmth, and lived in caves for shelter. They moved around looking for food and the other things they needed, and they only used things that were already there. They did not change the world around them very much.

Then, people in some parts of the world started growing plants and raising animals for food. Now they did not have to wander about all the time. They could stay in one place and build homes. By farming the land and building on it, they began to change the world around them. People have been changing the world ever since.

Plastics are used to make thousands of things in the home, from cups and beach balls to compact discs and the bodies of TV sets.

Computers now run many places, such as this solar power station. The most important parts of the computer are the tiny silicon chips.

Today we build cities with buildings so high they seem to touch the sky. We build dams across rivers to make huge lakes to store water. We use the water for drinking, washing, and making electricity. We build bridges and tunnels so that roads and railways can go over rivers and through mountains. We have found how to change our natural resources into metals, plastics, fabrics, glass, and concrete.

Our world is full of machines, and we couldn't live the way we do without them. Machines in factories make most of the things we use and wear. They sow and harvest our crops and milk our cows. They take us over land and sea, and through air and Space.

The Sun's family

We say that the Sun rises in the east and sets in the west. In fact, it is really the Earth that is moving, not the Sun. The Earth spins around in Space and makes the Sun look as if it is moving across the sky.

As it spins around, the Earth also moves in a big circle around the Sun. It takes a year to do this. The Earth is a **planet**, and there are eight other planets circling the Sun. The planets are the main part of the Sun's "family" in Space, which we call the Solar System.

4

3

2

1

Sun

1 Mercury
2 Venus
3 Earth
4 Mars
5 Jupiter
6 Saturn
7 Uranus

This photograph shows what the Sun looks like close up. It is boiling, bubbling hot gas all the way through.

5

6

7

The other planets are all very different from the Earth. There are no plants or animals on them, as there are on Earth. Two planets are closer to the Sun than the Earth, and they are too hot for anything to live. Six planets are farther from the Sun, and they are too cold. Only Earth is just right for living things.

These are seven of the planets in the Solar System, starting with the one nearest the Sun. Compare them with the size of the Earth, and see how much bigger or smaller each one is.

The biggest planet is Jupiter. It is a huge ball of cold gas, 11 times wider around the middle than the Earth.

The Sun is even bigger than Jupiter. It is a huge ball of gas, too, but in other ways it is quite different from Jupiter. Its gas is very hot, and gives out light and heat. Also, it is not a planet like Jupiter, but a **star** like the other stars in the sky. It only seems bigger and brighter than the others because it is much closer to us.

Moon and tides

Can you answer this riddle? What is the biggest yet the smallest thing you usually see in the sky at night?

The answer is the Moon. When we look at the Moon from Earth, it looks much bigger than the stars. In fact, it is really much smaller. It only looks bigger because it is closer to us than the stars.

The Moon is also much smaller than the Earth. If the Earth were the size of a football, the Moon would be the size of a tennis ball. But the Moon is like the Earth in one way. It is a ball of rock. We know this because astronauts have been to the Moon to find out.

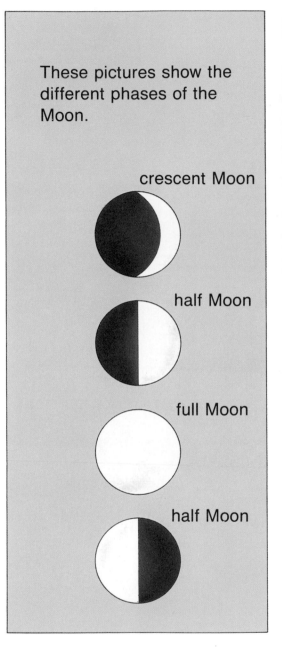

These pictures show the different phases of the Moon.

crescent Moon

half Moon

full Moon

half Moon

The Moon looks like this through a telescope. The dark patches are plains, the bright parts are mountains, and the circles are big holes, or craters.

If you look at the Moon at the same time for a few nights, you will see that it does not stay in the same place. This is because it is moving around the Earth. It takes about a month to do this.

Another thing you will see is that the Moon seems to change its shape. It will go from a thin line, or new Moon, to a curve, or crescent. Then it will grow to a half-circle, then a full circle, or full Moon. These changes happen each month, and are called the phases of the Moon.

The Moon only seems to change shape because of the way the Sun shines on it. It has no light of its own, it just reflects the light of the Sun. As the Moon moves around the Earth, the Sun shines on different parts and so makes its shape look different.

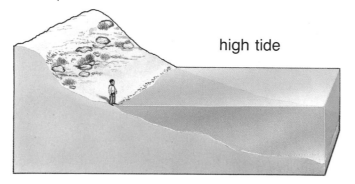

high tide

At the seashore, have you noticed how the sea comes in, then goes out? We call these movements the **tides**.

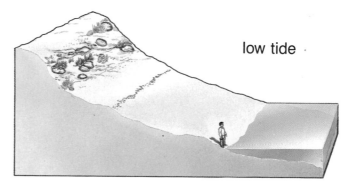

low tide

The Moon causes the tides. As it goes around the Earth, it pulls the water causing high and low tides.

Time

What time do you start school? Which month is your birthday? Which year were you born? We often need to know times and dates like these so that we can do the things we have to. We need a way of measuring, or splitting up, time. It must be the same for everybody. Just think what would happen if school started at 9 o'clock, but everybody's watch said a different time!

There are various things happening around us that we use to split up time. Our **day** is the length of time it takes the Earth to spin around once in Space. In that time, we have one sunrise, sunset, daytime, and nighttime.

On sundials like this, the shadow of the pointer in the middle shows what time it is.

This was an Egyptian water clock. It was filled with water at sunset and the water ran out slowly from a small hole. The level of the water marked the time of day.

Our **year** is the time it takes the Earth to go once around the Sun. The Moon takes just over 29 days to go through all its phases. This is roughly a month. A calendar shows all the days, weeks, and months in a year. There are 7 days in each week, and usually 365 days in a year. There are 12 months in each year.

As well as splitting time into days, months, and years, we split each day into hours and minutes. There are 24 hours in each day, and 60 minutes in each hour. We also split each day into two. From midnight to noon, there are 12 hours, and from noon to the next midnight, there are another 12 hours. After each half, we start counting the hours again, from 1 o'clock. This is why clock faces only need to show 12 hours.

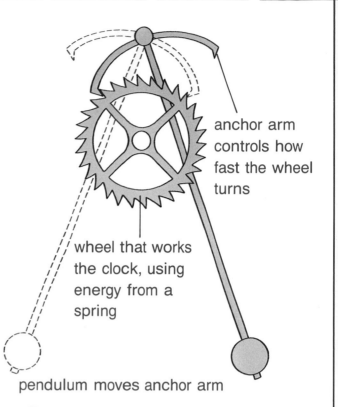

anchor arm controls how fast the wheel turns

wheel that works the clock, using energy from a spring

pendulum moves anchor arm

Some clocks have a pendulum that swings to and fro. Each swing takes the same time and keeps the clock right.

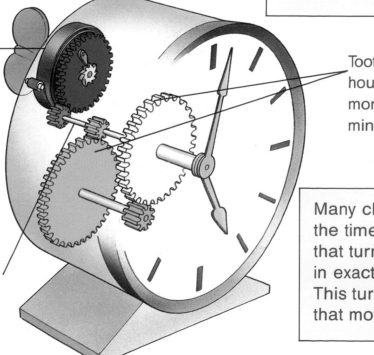

Spring stores energy which is used to turn the wheels. A balance wheel turns back and forth to control how much energy comes from the spring.

Central shaft turns the minute hand.

Toothed wheels turn the hour hand of the clock more slowly than the minute hand.

Many clocks measure the time with a wheel that turns back and forth in exactly the same time. This turns other wheels that move the hands.

The night sky

A clear sky at night is full of twinkling stars. These stars are just like our own Sun, but millions of times farther away. Many of these stars make patterns in the sky. Whenever you look, you will see the same patterns. We call them **constellations**.

Sometimes you see what look like very bright stars. The strange thing about them is that they are not always in the same place. This is because they are not stars, but planets, moving around the Sun.

You can see the planets Venus, Mars, and Jupiter easily on many nights of the year. Mars has a reddish-orange color. We call it the Red Planet. Venus is very bright, and you can often see it shining in the western sky, just after the Sun sets. We call it the Evening Star. You can also sometimes see it in the morning, just before sunrise, shining brightly in the east, and then we call it the Morning Star.

On some nights, you may see what look like stars shooting across the sky, or falling towards the Earth. These are not real stars but tiny bits of rock from outer Space burning up as they shoot through the sky. We call them **meteorites**.

You see different views of the constellations at different times of the year because the Earth is moving in Space. You might see the Plow constellation in either of these positions.

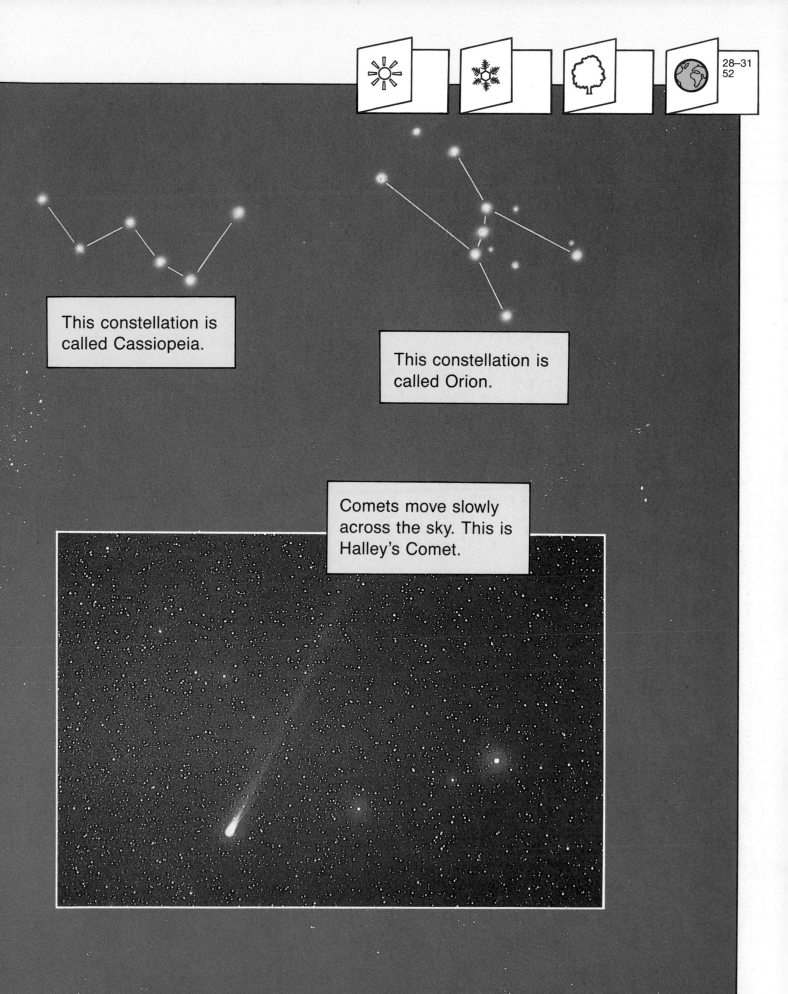

This constellation is called Cassiopeia.

This constellation is called Orion.

Comets move slowly across the sky. This is Halley's Comet.

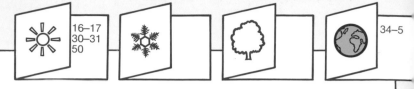

Using the stars

Every day the Sun rises in the east and sets in the west. We can use the Sun to help us find our way. Sailors often do this to find their way, or navigate, across the sea. They measure the position of the Sun in the sky at different times of the day. They know where the Sun should be at certain times and in certain places, so they can work out where they are.

Bees also find their way by using the Sun. So do some birds, which fly hundreds of miles every year in autumn and spring, on their way to and from warmer countries.

At night, both sailors and birds find their way by the stars. They know where different stars should be in the sky at different times, so they can tell their position just as they can from the Sun in the daytime.

Homing pigeons can fly hundreds of miles to reach their homes. They can work out the way to go from the Sun and stars.

light from Sun or star

mirror fixed to movable arm reflects Sun's image to line up with image of horizon

telescope

light from horizon

eye

This is a sextant. Sailors use it to measure where the Sun or a star is in the sky. Then they can work out which way to sail.

As the mirror is moved to line up the images of the Sun and the horizon, the end of the movable arm shows the position of the Sun above the horizon.

ACTIVITY CONTENTS

Each activity has a list of things you will need to do it, so find them and have them ready before you start.

Make sure you cover the table you're going to work on with old newspaper in case of any spills.

NEVER TASTE ANYTHING you are using, unless the book tells you to.

DON'T GO OUT ALONE TO SPOT STARS IN QUIET PLACES — go with a friend or, even better, a grown-up you know.

When the book tells you to get help from a grown-up, then do so, because on your own the activity might be dangerous.

Pressing air

Hold out your hand. Did you know that a weight is pressing on your hand? That is the pressure of the air above your hand. You don't feel it pressing because there is the same push from the air all around your hand, and this balances the push on any part of your hand.

Can you show that the air presses all ways on things?

- A glass
- A piece of cardboard bigger than the top of the glass

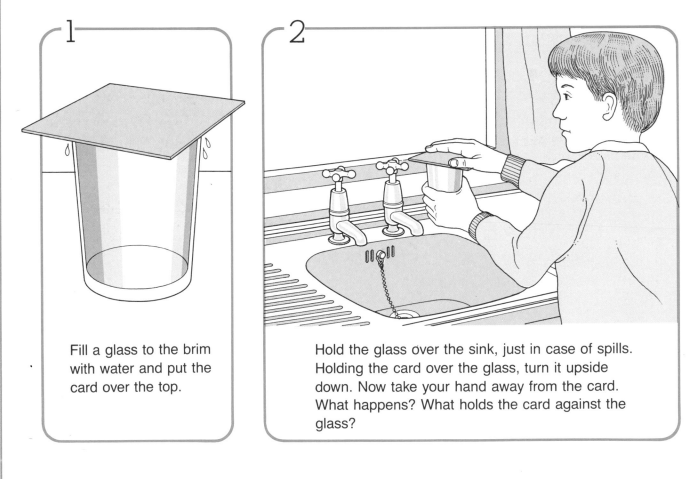

1 Fill a glass to the brim with water and put the card over the top.

2 Hold the glass over the sink, just in case of spills. Holding the card over the glass, turn it upside down. Now take your hand away from the card. What happens? What holds the card against the glass?

Which pushes harder, air or the water in the glass?

Strong paper?

Is a ruler stronger than paper? If you were asked that question, you would probably say "Yes." How can you make paper hold down a ruler?

- An old 12-inch ruler
- A sheet of newspaper

1 Put the ruler on a table with one end hanging about 4 inches over the edge.

2 Spread the sheet of newspaper over the ruler, right to the edge of the table. Smooth it down.

3 Hit the end of the ruler hard with your hand. What happens?

Did you expect the ruler to lift up the newspaper? Was it just the weight of the paper that held down the ruler, or was something else helping? See what happens if you use smaller and smaller sheets of paper. So, what do you think was helping to press the paper down on the ruler?

Give it a lift

Can you lift a piece of paper without using your hands?

- A strip of paper
- A thick book

1 Stand a book on end. Fix the piece of paper with one end between the pages of the book.

2 Now blow over the top of the book. What happens to the paper?

When you blow over the top of the paper, the air moves faster and so it doesn't push down as hard. But the air underneath is pushing up as usual and so it lifts the paper upward.

In the same way, the shape of an airplane wing makes the air move faster over the top of the wing. So what do you think happens when the plane starts to move fast? What makes the plane lift up off the ground?

A paper glider

Make your own plane or glider out of paper, and find out how to make it fly better.

- Sheets of paper
- Paper clips

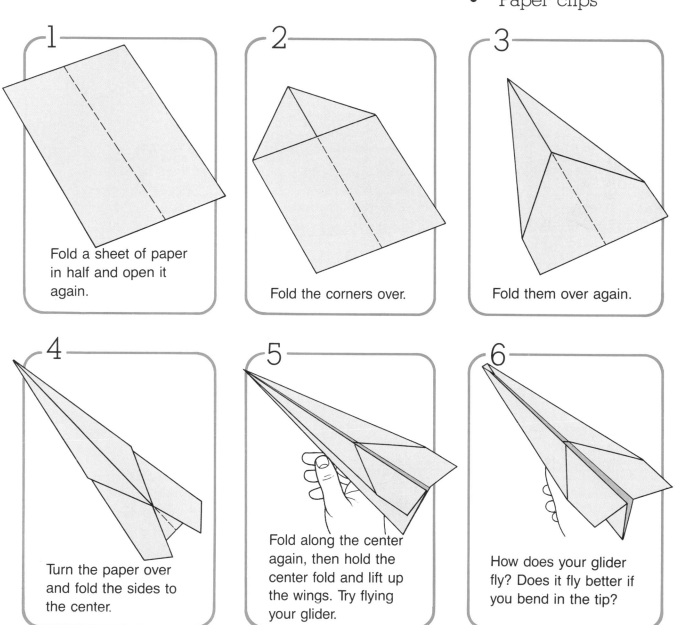

1 Fold a sheet of paper in half and open it again.

2 Fold the corners over.

3 Fold them over again.

4 Turn the paper over and fold the sides to the center.

5 Fold along the center again, then hold the center fold and lift up the wings. Try flying your glider.

6 How does your glider fly? Does it fly better if you bend in the tip?

Measure how far your glider flies. See if it flies better when you put paper clips on to weight the tip. Does it fly better or worse if you weight the tail with paper clips?

In control

Now you've made your glider, can you make it fly where you want it to?

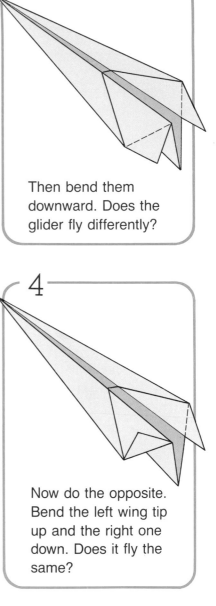

1 Try bending the ends of the wings. First bend them both upward. Then fly your glider. How does it go now?

2 Then bend them downward. Does the glider fly differently?

3 Now bend the left wing tip down and the right one up. What happens?

4 Now do the opposite. Bend the left wing tip up and the right one down. Does it fly the same?

Does the way you bend the tips of the wings make any difference? Which way do you bend them to make it fly up? Which way to make it fly down? How do you make it turn?

Real planes have moving parts on their wings to help them change direction when they are flying. If you fly in a plane, watch the parts move and see how the plane goes up, down, or turns.

A moving tail

Now try changing the design of your glider and see what happens.

- Scissors
- Paper
- Paper clips

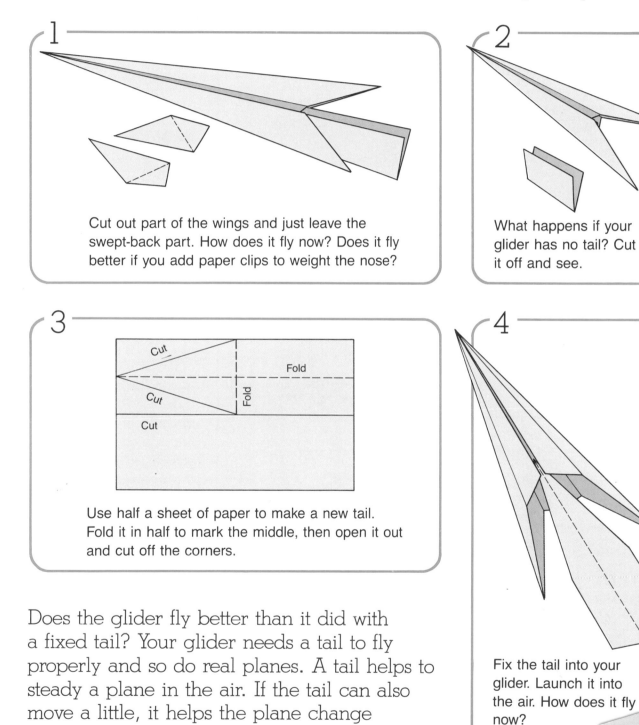

1

Cut out part of the wings and just leave the swept-back part. How does it fly now? Does it fly better if you add paper clips to weight the nose?

2

What happens if your glider has no tail? Cut it off and see.

3

Cut

Fold

Cut

Fold

Cut

Use half a sheet of paper to make a new tail. Fold it in half to mark the middle, then open it out and cut off the corners.

4

Fix the tail into your glider. Launch it into the air. How does it fly now?

Does the glider fly better than it did with a fixed tail? Your glider needs a tail to fly properly and so do real planes. A tail helps to steady a plane in the air. If the tail can also move a little, it helps the plane change direction.

Forecasting the weather

You don't need lots of equipment to try weather forecasting. All you need are your eyes and some things you can collect.

- Seaweed
- A pine cone
- A pin
- A straw

1 Next time you go to the seashore, bring back a long, flat piece of seaweed. Hang it up outside under shelter, and in the shade.

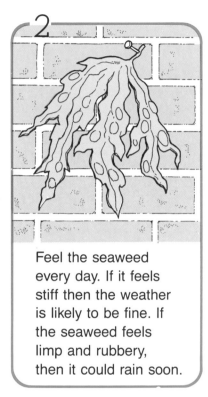

2 Feel the seaweed every day. If it feels stiff then the weather is likely to be fine. If the seaweed feels limp and rubbery, then it could rain soon.

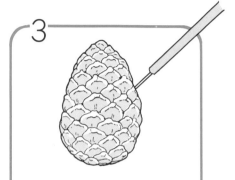

3 A pine cone works the same way. The scales close when the air is damp, and open when the air is dry. You can see the change more clearly if you stick a pin in one of the scales and put a straw on it to make a pointer. Put a piece of cardboard against the pine cone so that you can mark where the straw points.

People sometimes say things that forecast the weather. One is: "Red sky at night, sailor's delight: red sky in the morning, sailor's warning." What do you think this means? See if you can find out any other sayings that forecast the weather. Do any of them work?

Make your weather forecasts at the same time every day and write them down. Are they always right? Which give more forecasts that are right: the seaweed and pine cone, or the old sayings?

Clouds

Looking at the clouds can also give you an idea of how the weather may change.

1 Cumulus clouds

If the clouds look soft and fluffy like balls of cotton, the weather should stay fine.

2 Cumulonimbus clouds

But if they start getting blacker and taller, then rain is on its way.

3 Cirrus clouds

If you see wisps of cloud high up then the weather is going to change. These clouds are called "mares' " tails because they look like horses' tails.

Try making weather forecasts by looking at the clouds, and check to see if you were right.

Your weather station

All over the country there are weather stations where scientists use instruments to measure things about the weather.

You can make your own weather station in the yard. It is best to buy a simple thermometer to **measure the temperature**. But you can make other instruments yourself, and you can use your seaweed and pine cone to measure how damp the air is.

When you have set up your weather station, try to look at all your instruments once or twice a day, at the same time very day. Write down what they tell you. Note anything else about the weather you can think of. Is it sunny, cloudy, foggy, or frosty?

Measuring pressure

A barometer measures air pressure. Air pressure usually increases in fine weather and goes down before rain.

- A milk bottle
- A balloon
- Scissors
- An elastic band
- A straw
- Tape
- A piece of cardboard

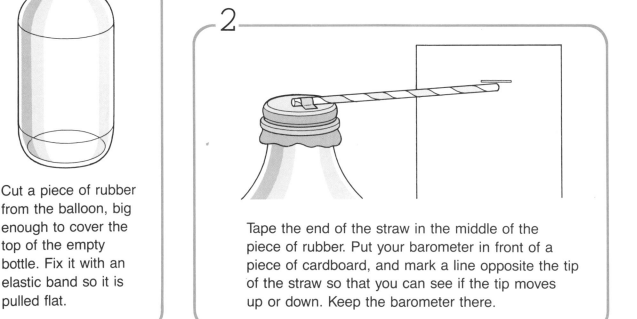

1 Cut a piece of rubber from the balloon, big enough to cover the top of the empty bottle. Fix it with an elastic band so it is pulled flat.

2 Tape the end of the straw in the middle of the piece of rubber. Put your barometer in front of a piece of cardboard, and mark a line opposite the tip of the straw so that you can see if the tip moves up or down. Keep the barometer there.

In fine weather, the air will press down harder on the piece of rubber, and the tip of the straw will move upward. When it rains, the tip of the straw will go down.

You should stand your barometer in a shady place. Can you think why? (See Moving Things page 9.)

Measuring rainfall

We measure rainfall in inches of water. It is the depth of rainwater which would be on the ground if it didn't run away. It is measured in a rain gauge.

- An empty paint can about 6 inches across
- A long straight stick or piece of wood
- A ruler

1

Stand the can in an open place outside. Make sure it is level and won't tip over.

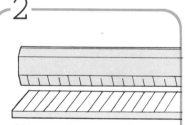

2

Use a ruler to make a scale to measure the depth of water in the can. Mark the piece of wood in quarter inches from 0–4 inches starting right from the end.

3

To measure the rainfall, make sure the can is level and then put your scale in it. Read off where the water comes to. Don't forget to "reset" your gauge afterwards by throwing away the water inside.

You can use other things to make a rain gauge but you must make sure the sides are upright all the way down and that the bottom is flat. Why do you think that is?

Catching the wind

You also need something to measure how hard the wind blows. This is called an anemometer. You will probably need help from a grown-up to make this.

- 3 yogurt cups the same size
- 3 knitting needles
- Scissors
- A cork
- A hammer and nail
- A large bead or two washers
- A thick stick or pole

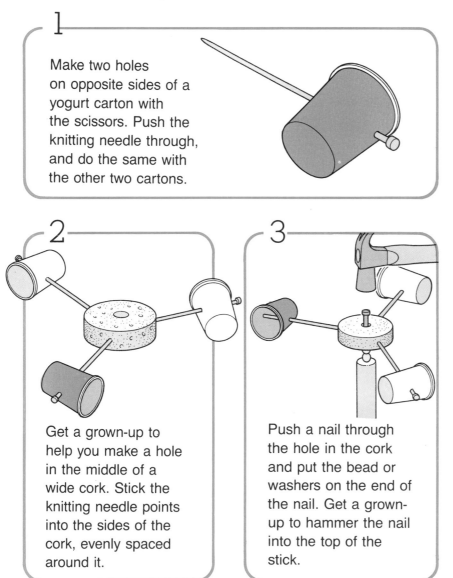

1 Make two holes on opposite sides of a yogurt carton with the scissors. Push the knitting needle through, and do the same with the other two cartons.

2 Get a grown-up to help you make a hole in the middle of a wide cork. Stick the knitting needle points into the sides of the cork, evenly spaced around it.

3 Push a nail through the hole in the cork and put the bead or washers on the end of the nail. Get a grown-up to hammer the nail into the top of the stick.

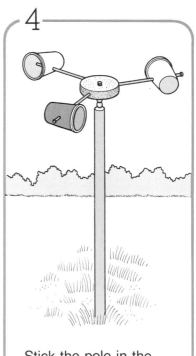

4 Stick the pole in the ground outside in an open space. Watch your anemometer spin around in the wind. The faster it spins, the stronger the wind.

How could you see how the wind changes from day to day? You could count how many turns your anemometer makes, but what else do you need to note while you're counting?

A wind vane

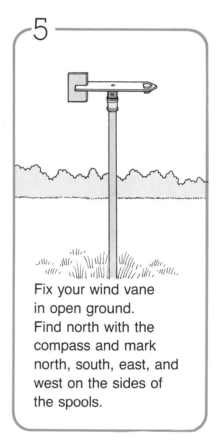

Another thing you should know is the direction in which the wind is blowing, so you need a wind vane. Remember that in the weather forecasts a north wind means one blowing from the north.

- Cardboard
- Scissors
- A stick or pole
- Glue
- A nail
- A bead
- Thread spools
- A compass
- A felt-tip pen

1

Cut out a strip of cardboard about 12 inches long and 1½ inches wide. Cut one end to a point and make a cut 1 inch deep into the other end. Cut another piece of cardboard about 6 inches by 3 inches. Make a cut 1 inch deep in the middle of one long side.

2

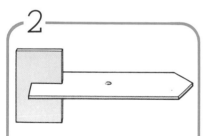

Slot the two pieces of cardboard together.

3

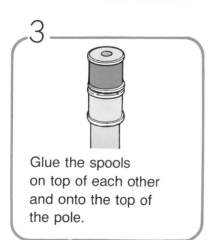

Glue the spools on top of each other and onto the top of the pole.

4

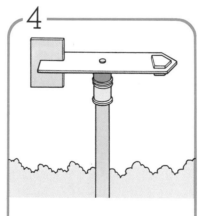

Push the nail through the middle of the strip of card and the bead, and stand the nail in the spools. You will probably have to glue some small pieces of cardboard at the pointed end of the cardboard strip to balance the tail.

5

Fix your wind vane in open ground. Find north with the compass and mark north, south, east, and west on the sides of the spools.

Does your wind vane face the wind or point in the same direction as the wind is traveling to?

Shadow clocks

The position of the Sun in the sky changes through the day, from the east in the morning to the west in the evening. So we could tell the time of day from the position of the Sun. BUT YOU MUST NOT LOOK DIRECTLY AT THE SUN BECAUSE IT WILL HURT YOUR EYES. Instead, you can tell where it is by looking at shadows.

- Chalk
- A stick 12 inches long
- Pointed pegs such as pot plant markers
- A felt-tip pen
- A compass

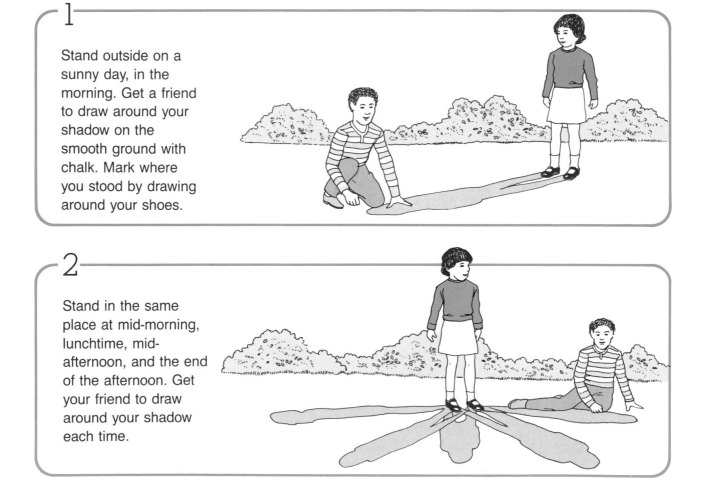

1 Stand outside on a sunny day, in the morning. Get a friend to draw around your shadow on the smooth ground with chalk. Mark where you stood by drawing around your shoes.

2 Stand in the same place at mid-morning, lunchtime, mid-afternoon, and the end of the afternoon. Get your friend to draw around your shadow each time.

What do you notice about your shadow? When is it shortest and when is it longest? Why do you think it changes? Think about the position of the Sun in the sky.

You can use shadows to make a clock.

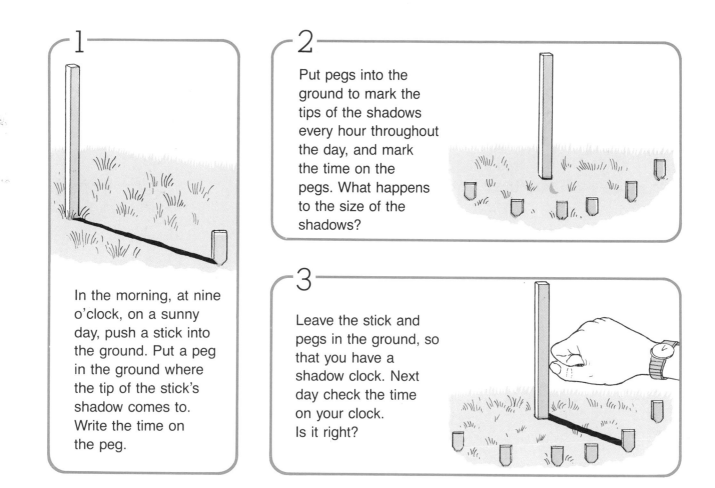

1

In the morning, at nine o'clock, on a sunny day, push a stick into the ground. Put a peg in the ground where the tip of the stick's shadow comes to. Write the time on the peg.

2

Put pegs into the ground to mark the tips of the shadows every hour throughout the day, and mark the time on the pegs. What happens to the size of the shadows?

3

Leave the stick and pegs in the ground, so that you have a shadow clock. Next day check the time on your clock. Is it right?

Use a compass to find out what direction the shadow is pointing in when it is shortest. Where must the Sun be, then?

Watch your clock for several weeks and see what happens to the shadows. It is best to look at the midday shadows. Measure how long they are on the first day of several months, and write down the measurements. When was the shadow longest; when was it shortest? Does this tell you anything about the Sun and the seasons?

The night sky

It is interesting and fun to find out about the stars in the night sky. One way you can do this is to make star maps that you can see in the dark. Make star maps from the ones in an astronomy book and then see if you can find the star patterns or constellations in the sky.

You must look at the right star maps in the book. The star patterns look different depending on whether you live in the northern or southern part of the world. So if you live in Europe or North America, you must look at the maps for the northern hemisphere. If you live in Australia or New Zealand, look at the ones for the southern hemisphere.

- Sheets of stiff black paper
- A flashlight
- A pin
- An astronomy book with star maps

1

Take a sheet of paper and get a friend to hold a flashlight underneath it. Make pin holes in the paper to copy the pattern of stars in the star maps. The light from the flashlight shines through the holes like stars.

2

On a clear dark night, dress warmly and go out with a friend to a place away from house and street lights. Let your eyes get used to the dark. Hold the flashlight under your star map and look for the patterns in the sky.

See if the constellations move around in the sky from month to month. You could try making your star maps while you're outdoors by making holes to copy patterns you can see in the sky. When you get home, see if you can match them with constellations in an astronomy book.

GLOSSARY

A glossary is a word list. This one explains the unusual words that are used in this book.

Air The mixture of gases that makes up the Earth's atmosphere. One of the main gases in it is oxygen.

Atmosphere The layer of air around the Earth.

Climate The kind of weather a country usually has.

Coal A fuel that we dig from the ground. It is the remains of huge plants that grew millions of years ago.

Constellations Patterns that stars make in the sky.

Continents The main land areas on the Earth. There are seven continents: Africa, Antarctica, Asia, Australia, Europe, North America, and South America.

Day The time it takes the Earth to spin around once in Space.

Deserts Places where little or no rain falls during the year. Deserts can be very hot all day, like the Sahara, or very cold, like the Antarctic.

Equator An imaginary line around the middle of the Earth.

Fuel Something that we burn to make heat. Coal, oil, and natural gas are our main fuels.

Hydro-electricity Electricity made by machines driven by flowing water. "Hydro" means "water."

Meteorite A piece of rock or metal from outer Space that may burn up as it passes through the Earth's atmosphere. The streak of light this makes is called a meteor.

Minerals Materials that we mine, or dig from the ground.

Natural gas One of our main fuels. We find it trapped in underground rocks.

Natural resources The things we get from nature, which help us live the way we do.

Oil Our most important fuel. We get it by drilling into the rocks.

Oxygen The gas in the air which we must breathe to live.

Petroleum Another name for oil. The word means "rock oil."

Planet A body that circles in Space around the Sun. The Earth is one of nine planets.

Poles Points on the "top" and "bottom" of the Earth as it spins in Space. There is a North Pole and a South Pole.

Seasons Times of the year that have different kinds of weather. Many places have four seasons — winter, spring, summer, and autumn.

Solar power Power that we get from the Sun.

Solar System The Sun's family in Space. The planets are the main part of the Solar System.

Space It begins high above the Earth where there is no air. The Earth, the Sun, and everything we see in the night sky are traveling through Space.

Stars Huge balls of very hot gas, which give out light and heat. The Sun is our star.

Tides The daily rise and fall of the water in the oceans. They are caused by the gravity, or pull of the Moon.

Water vapor Water that has turned to gas in the air.

Wings The parts of a bird or a plane that keep it up in the air.

Year The time it takes the Earth to travel once around the Sun in Space.

INDEX

The **dark** numbers tell you where you will find a picture of the subject.